# Swimming
# & diving

# the

# SUMMER OLYMPICS

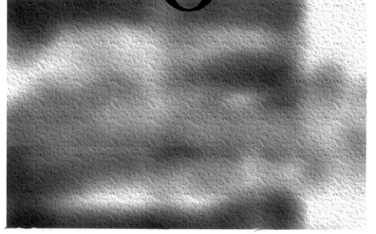

# *S*wimming & diving

SUMMER OLYMPICS

**PUBLISHED BY SMART APPLE MEDIA**

Published by Smart Apple Media
123 South Broad Street, Mankato, Minnesota 56001

Cover Illustration by Eric Melhorn

Designed by Core Design

Photos by: Allsport, Bettmann Archives and Wide World
Photos

**Library of Congress Cataloging-in-Publication Data**

Smale, David.
Swimming and diving / by David Smale.
(The Summer Olympics)
Includes index.
Summary: Provides an overview of swimming and diving
competitions at the Olympics.

**ISBN 1-887068-08-2**

1. Swimming—Juvenile literature. 2. Diving—Juvenile
literature. 3. Olympics—Juvenile literature. [1. Swimming—History. 2. Diving—History. 3. Olympics.] I. Title.
II. Series.

GV837.S727  1995              95-11969
797.21—dc20

## A FAVORITE PASTIME

People seem to have a natural affinity for water. In warm weather, ocean beaches are crowded with people seeking surf and sun. Swimming pools dot neighborhoods throughout the world. In some areas, the local swimming hole is a lake or stream, where children and adults alike swim and play.

It's no wonder, then, that sporting events involving water

*Diving demands perfect execution and control.*

*Alfred Hajós survived the early Olympics in good style.*

are extremely popular. Every four years when the Olympics roll around, the swimming and diving venues are among the most widely watched. It seems there's always a big story in the swimming pool. Whether it's an aging veteran making one last drive for a medal or a freckle-faced kid making a big splash on the international scene, the pool is a hot spot in Olympic competition. And with the 1996 Olympics in Atlanta quickly approaching, the world waits to see the next star.

## FROM RIVERS TO POOLS

Men's swimming competition began in 1896 in Athens, the first time the modern-day Olympics were held. The women had their first swimming competition in 1912 in Stockholm. In these early Olympics, competitions were usually held in natural bodies of water. For example, in Athens in 1896, the swimming competition was held in the Bay of Zea. Bad weather conditions made the competition difficult. The water temperature was just 55 degrees (13 °C) and the waves crested at 12 feet (3.66m). Hungarian Alfred Hajós, who won two of the three races contested (100- and 1,200-meter freestyle), said that his primary goal was survival, not winning.

In Paris in 1900, the competition was held in the River Seine. That year, times were faster than usual as the athletes swam with the current.

*A close race in women's freestyle competition (pages 10-11).*

More consistent use of man-made pools later in that decade meant that times began to get much better and the capability of including more and longer events was increased.

Currently, for both men and women, there are 18 swimming and diving events being contested at the Olympics. The individual races consist of the following: five freestyle (50, 100, 200, 400 and 1,500 meters); two breaststroke (100 and 200 meters); two butter-

*Reaching for the water in top form.*

fly (100 and 200 meters); two backstroke (100 and 200 meters); and two individual medley (200 and 400 meters). The individual medley includes equal legs in the butterfly, backstroke, breaststroke and freestyle.

In addition, there are two freestyle relays (4 x 100 and 4 x 200) and the 4 x 100-meter medley relay. In the relays, four contestants from each team swim equal distances consecutively.

The diving events are the 3-meter springboard and the 10-meter platform. The springboard is a movable, flexible board that propels the diver into the air, while the platform is an immovable slab from which the diver provides all the propulsion.

*Buster Crabbe was a powerful freestyler in the 1932 Olympics.*

## STROKE, STROKE, STROKE

The freestyle is the fastest and most common stroke in swimming. Most beginning swimmers learn the freestyle method first. In this stroke, the swimmer brings the arms over the shoulders and pulls the body through the water. The backstroke is similar except the swimmer is floating on his or her back.

The most complicated stroke is the breaststroke. In this stroke, the swimmer must: 1) make all leg and arm movements

*Janet Evans (above) reaches for victory with a strong backstroke.*

simultaneously; 2) keep both shoulders in line with the water; 3) push both hands forward from the breast and bring them back on or under the water; 4) use the backward-and-out frog-leg kick; 5) touch hands simultaneously to the wall on all turns and the finish; and 6) keep the head above water at all times except for the start and the first stroke and kick from each turn.

The butterfly stroke is a variation of the breaststroke. Before the third rule for the breaststroke was instituted, American swimmers were bringing their arms out of the water on the return stroke, which saved time and energy. This developed into the butterfly stroke, which became a separate Olympic event in 1952. The new stroke also allows an up-and-down kick.

## MEN'S SWIMMING: A LONG LINE OF WINNERS

Through the years, American men have dominated the swimming competition with few exceptions. Other countries have had individual champions who have done well, but no country has had a line of champions that compares with the United States. The first American swimming star was Duke Paoa Kahinu Makoe Hulikohoa Kahanamoku. Kahanamoku, who was born in Hawaii, won three gold and two silver medals in four different Olympics beginning in 1912.

The next great American champion was Johnny Weissmuller. Weissmuller won five gold medals in 1924 and 1928, and also

claimed a bronze medal as a member of the U.S. water polo team.
Weissmuller went on to star in 12 Hollywood films as Tarzan.
Buster Crabbe, who won the gold medal in the 400-meter
freestyle in the 1932 Olympics in Los Angeles, also became a
famous movie star, portraying such characters as Tarzan, Buck
Rogers and Flash Gordon.

    In 1964 American Don Schollander became the first swim-

*Johnny Weissmuller -- from Olympic champion to Tarzan.*

mer to win four gold medals in one Olympics. But no one has matched the record of Mark Spitz. Spitz was entered in seven events in the Munich Games in 1972. He hoped to become the first Olympian in any sport to win seven gold medals in one Olympics. And he did it, winning gold medals in the 200-meter butterfly, the 4 x 100-meter freestyle relay, the 200-meter freestyle, the 100-meter butterfly, the 4 x 200-meter freestyle relay, the 100-meter freestyle and the medley relay. His record still stands as the greatest individual medal achievement in one Olympics.

American Matt Biondi had the opportunity to duplicate Spitz's effort in the 1988 Games in Seoul when he was entered in seven events. He fell short, but just barely, winning five gold medals and two silvers. He then came back to win one more gold and a silver in the 1992 Games in Barcelona. That year Biondi was part of the most dominating team performance in Olympic swimming competition. The United States won 27 medals—11 gold, nine silver and seven bronze. The team with the next highest total was Germany, with 11 medals.

## WOMEN'S SWIMMING: TWO STRONG NATIONS

Over the past 20 years, the women's swimming competition has been dominated by the East Germans and the Americans. The East Germans first came into prominence in 1976.

Kornelia Ender, who won gold medals in the 100- and 200-meter freestyles, the 100-meter butterfly and the 4 x 100 medley relay, was part of an amazing team that won 11 of the 13 events contested in Montreal. The only event the East German team did not medal in was the 200-meter breaststroke.

As late as 1988, the East Germans still were doing well. Kristin Otto won an amazing six gold medals, and Heike Friedrich,

*Women's diving is a tremendous display of strength and form.*

who had won 14 consecutive finals in world championship competition, claimed the gold in the 200-meter freestyle.

There was another star that year, however. Krisztina Egerszegi of Hungary broke onto the scene, becoming the youngest Olympic swimming champion in history when, at age 14, she won the 200-meter backstroke. Four years later she claimed gold in the 100- and 200-meter backstroke and the 400-meter individual medley.

The United States has also had numerous stars, such as Mary Meagher, who won three gold medals in the Los Angeles Games in 1984. But few swimming stars have enjoyed the popularity of Janet Evans. Evans was a 17-year-old high school student when she earned gold medals in the 400- and 800-meter freestyle events

*Mark Spitz (above) and Greg Louganis (right) - two Olympic stars.*

*Sometimes victory brings new world-record times.*

and the 400-meter individual medley in Seoul in 1988. Her enthusiastic smile captured the nation's attention. Four years later, the young veteran repeated her victory in the 800-meter freestyle.

## BARELY A SPLASH

Divers earn gold medals based on how perfectly they perform their dives, a more subjective method than comparing times. One of the critical elements of a perfect dive is a lack of splash. It is a thing of beauty when an athlete enters the pool from high above the surface and barely makes a ripple in the water.

Because of their grace and daring, divers have often captured the world's attention. The first big celebrity off the men's diving board was Klaus Dibiasi of Italy. Dibiasi claimed the silver medal in 1964 in the 10-meter platform diving. He came back to win three consecutive gold medals from 1968 through 1976.

Dibiasi then passed the crown to American Greg Louganis. Louganis was 16 years old in 1976 and finished second in the platform and sixth in the springboard. The U.S. boycott of the 1980 Olympics in Moscow kept Louganis from competing, but he then won the gold in both the springboard and the 10-meter platform in Los Angeles in 1984.

In 1988, the aging veteran nearly was dethroned by the platform itself. During the preliminary round, Louganis hit his head on the cement platform during a back flip. But he overcame the

*The butterfly stroke (pages 26-27).*

injury and the low point total to earn another gold in the platform. He also repeated his gold in the springboard.

The American women practically owned 3-meter springboard diving between 1920 and 1948. During that span, the United States won *every medal* in the event. Madeleine Moreau of France was the first non-American to earn a medal in the event when she claimed the silver medal in 1952. Ingrid Krämer of East Germany was the first non-American woman to win a gold medal in the event when she won back-to-back golds in 1960 and 1964.

Pat McCormick was one of America's first female diving stars. She won both diving competitions in the 1952 Games in Helsinki. She came back in 1956 in Melbourne, eight months after giving birth to her son, and duplicated her effort. Her second child, daughter Kelly, also earned Olympic fame in the springboard competition by taking the silver in 1984 and the bronze in 1988.

## MORE COMPETITION AHEAD

For the second time in 12 years, the Olympics will return to American soil. The 1996 Games in Atlanta should provide plenty of excitement for swimming and diving fans. But who will be the main competitors?

The unification of Germany made for a very strong team in 1992, and the Germans should continue to be strong com-

petitors. The breakup of the Soviet Union, which won 10 medals in 1992, will likely have a far-reaching effect. China has been gaining on the rest of the world with amazing speed, despite repeated accusations of abuse of performance-enhancing drugs. The Chinese women won their first four swimming gold medals and three diving golds in their history in 1992, and today, many of the world records belong to the Chinese women. Then there are the Americans, who always field a strong team. With the competition in their own backyard pool, lots of medals are expected.

Of course, there's always a surprise at the next flip turn.

*The top athletes are poised to capture many medals in Atlanta.*

# swimming & diving

**RECORDS**

Men's Swimming Competition (Olympic Record Holders)

| Event | Record Holder (country) | Time (min:sec) |
|---|---|---|
| 50-meter freestyle | Alexander Popov (Unified Team) | 0:21.91 |
| 100-meter freestyle | Matt Biondi (USA) | 0:48.63 |
| 200-meter freestyle | Evgueni Sadovyi (Unified Team) | 1:46.70 |
| 400-meter freestyle | Evgueni Sadovyi (Unified Team) | 3:45.00 |
| 1500-meter freestyle | Kieren Perkins (Australia) | 14:43.48 |
| 100-meter backstroke | Mark Tewksbury (Canada) | 0:53.98 |
| 200-meter backstroke | Martin Lopez-Zubero (Spain) | 1:58.47 |
| 100-meter breaststroke | Nelson Diebel (USA) | 1:01.50 |
| 200-meter breaststroke | Mike Barrowman (USA) | 2:10.16 |
| 100-meter butterfly | Anthony Nesty (Suriname) | 0:53.00 |
| 200-meter butterfly | Melvin Stewart (USA) | 1:56.26 |
| 200-meter ind. medley | Tamas Darnyi (Hungary) | 2:00.17 |
| 400-meter ind. medley | Tamas Darnyi (Hungary) | 4:14.23 |
| 4 x 100-meter freestyle relay | Jacobs,Dalbey, Jager, Biondi (USA) | 3:16.53 |
| 4 x 200-meter freestyle relay | Lepikov, Pychnenko, Taianovitch,Sadovyi (Unified Team) | 7:11.95 |
| 4 x 100-meter medley relay | Rouse,Diebel, Morales, Olsen (USA) | 3:36.93 |

Men's Diving Competition (Gold Medal Winners)

| Year | Springboard Diving Diver | Country | Platform Diving Diver | Country |
|---|---|---|---|---|
| 1904 | (no competition) | | G E. Sheldon | USA |
| 1908 | Albert Zürner | Germany | Hjalmar Johansson | Sweden |
| 1912 | Paul Günther | Germany | Erik Adlerz | Sweden |
| 1920 | Louis Kuehn | USA | Clarence Pinkston | USA |
| 1924 | Albert White | USA | Albert White | USA |
| 1928 | Pete Desjardins | USA | Pete Desjardins | USA |
| 1932 | Michael Galitzen | USA | Harold Smith | USA |
| 1936 | Richard Degener | USA | Marshall Wayne | USA |
| 1948 | Bruce Harlan | USA | Samuel Lee | USA |
| 1952 | David Browning | USA | Samuel Lee | USA |
| 1956 | Robert Clotworthy | USA | Joaquin Capilla | Mexico |
| 1960 | Gary Tobian | USA | Robert Webster | USA |
| 1964 | Ken Sitzberger | USA | Robert Webster | USA |
| 1968 | Bernard Wrightson | USA | Klaus Dibiasi | Italy |
| 1972 | Vladimir Vasin | USSR | Klaus Dibiasi | Italy |
| 1976 | Phil Boggs | USA | Klaus Dibiasi | Italy |
| 1980 | Aleksandr Portnov | USSR | Falk Hoffmann | E.Germany |
| 1984 | Greg Louganis | USA | Greg Louganis | USA |
| 1988 | Greg Louganis | USA | Greg Louganis | USA |
| 1992 | Mark Lenzi | USA | Sun Shuwei | China |

# swimming & diving

Women's Swimming Competition (Olympic Record Holders)

| Event | Record Holder (country) | Time (min:sec) |
|---|---|---|
| 50-meter freestyle | Yang Wenyi (China) | 0:24.79 |
| 100-meter freestyle | Zhuang Yong (China) | 0:54.65 |
| 200-meter freestyle | Heike Friedrich (E. Germany) | 1:57.65 |
| 400-meter freestyle | Janet Evans (USA) | 4:03.85 |
| 800-meter freestyle | Janet Evans (USA) | 8:20.20 |
| 100-meter backstroke | Krisztina Egerszegi (Hungary) | 1:00.68 |
| 200-meter backstroke | Krisztina Egerszegi (Hungary) | 2:07.06 |
| 100-meter breaststroke | Tania Dangalakova (Bulgaria) | 1:07.95 |
| 200-meter breaststroke | Kyoko Iwasaki (Japan) | 2:26.65 |
| 100-meter butterfly | Quian Hong (China) | 0:58.62 |
| 200-meter butterfly | Mary T. Meagher (USA) | 2:06.90 |
| 200-meter ind. medley | Lin Li (China) | 2:11.65 |
| 400-meter ind. medley | Petra Schneider (E. Germany) | 4:36.29 |
| 4 x 100-meter freestyle relay | Haislett, Torres, Martino, Thompson (USA) | 3:39.46 |
| 4 x 100-meter medley relay | Loveless, Nall, Ahmann-Leighton, Thompson (USA) | 4:02.54 |

Women's Diving Competition (Gold medal winners)

| Year | Springboard Diving Diver | Country | Platform Diving Diver | Country |
|---|---|---|---|---|
| 1912 | — | — | Greta Johansson | Sweden |
| 1920 | Aileen Riggin | USA | Stefani Fryland-Clausen | Denmark |
| 1924 | Elizabeth Becker | USA | Caroline Smith | USA |
| 1928 | Helen Meany | USA | Elizabeth Pinkston | USA |
| 1932 | Georgia Coleman | USA | Dorothy Poynton | USA |
| 1936 | Marjorie Gestring | USA | Dorothy Poynton-Hill | USA |
| 1948 | Victoria Draves | USA | Victoria Draves | USA |
| 1952 | Patricia McCormick | USA | Patricia McCormick | USA |
| 1956 | Patricia McCormick | USA | Patricia McCormick | USA |
| 1960 | Ingrid Krämer | E. Germany | Ingrid Krämer | E. Germany |
| 1964 | Ingrid Engel-Krämer | E. Germany | Lesley Bush | USA |
| 1968 | Sue Gossick | USA | Milena Duchková | Czech. |
| 1972 | Micki King | USA | Ulrika Knape | Sweden |
| 1976 | Jennifer Chandler | USA | Elena Vaytsekhovskaya | USSR |
| 1980 | Irina Kalinina | USSR | Martina Jäschke | E. Germany |
| 1984 | Sylvie Bernier | Canada | Zhou Jihong | China |
| 1988 | Gao Min | China | Xu Yanmei | China |
| 1992 | Gao Min | China | Fu Mingxia | China |

INDEX